The Last War

Poetry about War and PTSD

MICHAEL F. MORTON

Angels Three Productions

Copyright © 2017 Michael F. Morton

All rights reserved.

ISBN-13: 978-0-9995832-2-7

DEDICATION

For love of Country,
To those who serve, have and will serve, and the families that support them

Thank you, Michael.

TO

My Angels 3

Michelle, Megan and Tristan

To my Brothers,

RAIDERS FOR LIFE

CONTENTS

   Acknowledgments   i

1   Poetry about War and PTSD   3

ACKNOWLEDGMENTS

Thank you to those who believed in me and my writing. You pushed me to get my works published, even when I didn't think it was good.

1 POETRY OF WAR AND PTSD

MICHAEL F. MORTON

Return To Innocence

Your darkness does exist,
You must recognize it,
But only as you focus on remembering the good,
In your journey to return to innocence,

A return to Innocence signifies,
We have faith in ourselves and others,
It allows us to be vulnerable,
And open without fear,

When you return to Innocence,
You will find your source of inner strength,
An inherent wisdom and healing,
A new life is waiting for you to take the first step,

The eyes of truth are always watching,
The past and future are only in your imagination,
The present moment,
Is the only one that never ends,

It takes courage to question yourself,
You will never find the light with your eyes closed,
You will never find your peace,
By dwelling on your mistakes,

Just look inside your heart,
Don't be afraid to be exposed,
Don't let pride,
Build a prison from which there is no escape,

Give thanks for every moment,
Every breath, every fault,
Every laugh, every sigh,
Every chance is a new chance in life,

The beginning of your tomorrow starts today,
Every step is a step forward,
Don't let pride keep your words,

THE LAST WAR

Embrace humility and admit when you need help,

Return to innocence and see the world in everything around you,
The beauty of a rainy day,
Hold endlessness in your heart,
And an eternity of love for all.

I finished this poem on 21 May 2015. The inspiration for this poem came from talking with Veterans, and their recognizing they have PTSD. Finding peace from PTSD is a journey, a journey to find your true self. The innocence that was you before war.

Behind the Stone

        Behind the Stone of polished black,
    A clouded reflection of war long forgotten,
Row upon row, names of the departed are etched for all time,
     A black scar rising upon the history of man,

          Behind the Stone,
     Many a life will never be known,
   Dreams cut short by the delusion of man,
    Dreams that remain sealed forever,

          Behind the Stone,
   Faces look out at the faces looking in,
     Both faces searching for hope,
    Watching, waiting to be remembered,

          Behind the Stone.
    Cracks form by the tears of many,
  Those in front attempt to mend the wounds,
Placing symbols of healing within the fractured blackness,

      Masses gather to the Stone,
To touch once again their memories of a different time,
Tears are laid upon those names read and remembered,
     But many yet will go unspoken,

          Behind the Stone,
   The dead have seen the end of war,
   Those that face the polished black,
  Have been dying since coming home,

The Stone of polished black is not a memorial of war,
       But a memorial to life,
    For the Stone remembers their names,
     And the Stone never forgets.

I finished this poem on 21 May 2015. The inspiration for this poem came from talking with a support group of Vietnam Veterans. They were having a Vietnam Veterans reunion and I was asked to write a poem for them. I used the Vietnam War Memorial (The Wall), as a symbol to highlight the sacrifices our Vietnam Veterans made for our freedom.

THE LAST WAR

Open Your Eyes

Leaving without a sound,
Not even a chance to say why,
Engulfed by the darkness,
Only you could have seen,

Now a single rose I lay,
As the tears fall from my face,
It's a cold day to say goodbye,
If only you could have seen,

A permanent solution,
To a temporary problem,
You were laid to rest,
As we are left holding on to yesterday,

Open your eyes,
See the world and your tomorrow,
Your candle has been lite,
Its ok to leave the pain behind,

Stand up,
No need to drown in the past,
No need to wander in the dark,
There is no solution on the other side,

Take my hand,
I will keep you clear and calm,
A lifetime of possibilities,
Waits in front of you,

This can be the first day of your life,
To find the peace you need to find,
You have the power to heal your wounded heart,
Just Open Your Eyes

I finished this poem on 21 May 2015. The inspiration for this poem came from hearing another Veteran had committed suicide, as they were struggling with PTSD. I have lost a few brothers to this horrible tragedy. Those who are suffering with PTSD are wandering around in the dark. A darkness you cannot see. They need help to see there is a tomorrow, that they can leave the pain behind. If they open their eyes, get them to see they need help and they get it, they can find the first day of their new life. Suicide is a permanent solution to a temporary problem.

The Disease

In thunderous silences,
The Disease does sound its trumpet,
Echoing through the veins,
Of those who hear its call,

The disease does not value life,
It feeds on the decay of the soul,
Only life can value life,
And only life can see its truth,

On hollowed breath,
The Disease speaks against the grains of truth,
Which settle on the tongue,
Siphoning the meaning from melting hearts,

Shrouding the heart in obscurity,
Destroying the tenets structure within,
Engulfing the reason,
With walls of hopelessness,

The innocent sees no more,
The Disease will not perceive the certainty,
Nor hear the whisper of care,
Over the lullaby symphony playing in silent,

Hearts fil with sadness,
As the lie tells another lie,
Warping and twisting the conviction,
Taking what is not to be taken,

Do not let it in,
Do not listen to the lies it tells,
Find in you the reason to be found,
And shed the light on all the ones who never thought they could see.

I finished this poem on 9 September 2015. The inspiration for this poem came from talking with some combat veterans about the rising numbers of suicides. Suicide is a disease that imprisons the soul. It builds a wall around your heart, and engulfs you into darkness. The current suicide rate amongst veterans today (September 2017) is an average of 22 per day. Suicide is a lie, it tells you everything will be better, the pain will go away. But the truth is, those that commit suicide pass their pain onto their family and friends. They are left holding on to the victim's tomorrows, with an eternity of empty answers.

The Crucible

The Crucible,
The test of tests,
Once you've started,
Never will it end,

The erosion of creation,
The destroyer of the dream that is peace,
The blood-stained world,
Forever weeps in ferocious silence,

Forged in the Crucible,
Are a Brothers bond,
Brothers in Arms,
A bond that will see no end,

Mourning the loss of One,
Is a heartache like no other,
A pain that reaches the soul,
An infinite stain of sorrow,

The Crucible invades your dreams,
A living hell of nightmares,
The screams of the fallen,
The faces that never look away,

The distant cries of the innocent,
Echo throughout all time,
As the days ever so hopelessly drift away,
The unforgiving lies spread upon the winds,

The Crucible will forever change you,
Deep within your core,
Causing the strongest,
To live with fear and regret,

The Crucible is now,
It is everywhere and forever,
Look no further than your mind,

For the shadows of the test have consumed you.

I finished this poem on 24 March 2015. The inspiration for this poem came from talking with combat Veterans about war. War is only about death. Those that have been to war, will forever be bonded together. War changes you forever, and many times it's not for the good. These changes do not go away. You must find a way out of the darkness, make friends with the faces in your dreams and ask for help. Seeking help is not a sign of weakness my brothers and sisters. I did!

Lifeless Eyes

Into those eyes,
Lifeless and dark,
No truth, no lies,
Only tormented years of numbing pain,

They see into nothingness,
Bended,
Drained,
Enslaved,

A mind trapped inside the trauma,
Here, but still there,
Searching for an open door,
Looking for a tomorrow without fear,

So many images absorbed,
A mind mazed with mirrored walls,
Trapped within a silent prison,
Into a purple haze of nothingness,

Noises replay the frightening scenes,
As haunting cries engulf the body,
All that is hell,
There is no escape,

Hardened of heart,
Confined within the fury,
Drowning in memories,
Buried deep within the soul,

Behind those lifeless eyes,
A broken life and shattered mind,
Tears fall from untold scars,
As darkness suffocates the broken truth

I finished this poem on 19 June 2017. The inspiration for this poem came from visiting with some combat veterans during a Wounded Warrior event. I could tell one of the Veterans was really having a hard time with the crowd and loud noise. He never said a word, but his eyes spoke volumes. He was there, but he really wasn't there. Only because I have been there, could I recognize his trauma. PTSD is wound you cannot see, and it cannot be fixed by a few simple counseling sessions. That would be like trying to dam Niagara Falls with a Solo cup. The healing from PTSD takes time, and it cannot be measured by a calendar. If you have never served in the military or been to combat, you may not understand the complexity of what they are going through. If you know someone who is struggling with PTSD, the best advice I can offer is to just simply tell them you care, and you are there to listen. They may open up to you or they may not. But they will hear you.

Sidelines

So you think you're on the sidelines,
Watching all that is life go by,
Placed there by your unique challenges,
Confined only by your consciousness,

You think you've lost everything,
But you have so much more,
In your heart lies the spark,
In your soul burns the will,

Your challenges are a gift,
A gift that makes you strong enough to overcome it,
Smart enough to figure it out,
And brave enough to use it,

You can endure overwhelming obstacles,
If your belief becomes your conviction,
Obstacles are placed in our paths not to stop us,
But to ignite our strength and courage,

Don't confine your spirit,
Even if you only do one thing well,
You are needed by others,
More than you know,

The journey starts with one belief,
By doing what is necessary,
By doing what is possible,
And soon you are doing the impossible,

The human spirit is one of ability,
Resiliency and courage that no challenge can steal away,
Face the Sunshine,
And your shadows will fall behind.

I finished this poem on 25 May 2017. The inspiration for this poem came from hearing combat Veterans talk about their disabilities. Some of these Veterans have lost limbs, sight, or some with wounds you cannot see. Small minorities of Veterans with these disabilities hide behind them, or use them as an excuse to not move forward in life. The truth is, the only limitations you have are the ones you place upon yourself. During one of my combat tours in Iraq, we hit an IED (Roadside bomb) and it destroyed our HUMMV. We all sustained injuries, but the driver of the truck ended up losing both his legs due to being badly burned. I struggled with the guilt of being the leader and not being able to save him. I was hurt badly, my back and neck, but was able to walk and move around. I felt sorry for myself, and yet he was hurt far worse than I was. He received great treatment at the Army hospital in San Antonio, and I was told many times that he was up and moving around in a wheelchair. Going to visit other wounded veterans, motivating them to get up and start moving. He refused to sit on the sidelines; he was alive, and going to be alive in life. That's when I stood up and said no more! I am going to sit on the sidelines, and watch life go by.

MICHAEL F. MORTON

War In Peace

I yearned so long,
To finally make it home,
My duty done,
To find my peace from war,

I thought my war had ended,
But my eyes tell a different tale,

I see into nothingness,
My mind bended,
My peace enslaved,
My nightmare begun,

Fires rage,
Screams of pain,
Cries for help,
The smell of death surrounds me,

I can see their faces,
The dead and wounded,
Those heroes known,
And those I didn't,

I fight to succumb,
My mind drained dry,
The pestilence fear overwhelming,

Prayers for deliverance I try,
Senseless numbing no resolve,
My fate uncertain,
My destiny unknown,

As long as the war is alive in me,
My wounds do not heal,
No peace I find,

Hear me,
My family and comrades,

THE LAST WAR

This fate I have assigned,

To find peace,
Peace for us,
And those like us,

Death is a fact of War,
And wounds will heal in time,
But no one returns unwounded,

I finished this poem on 24 April 2015. The inspiration for this poem came from talking with fellow students in my Master's program at the time. The subject obviously was PTSD, and the difficulties that veterans have expressing their thoughts and feelings about their experiences. So I wrote this from the Veterans perspective, my perspective at one time. Those that have been to war, want peace more than anything else in their lives, and that peace can come in many different forms. Some will use alcohol or drugs to find it; others will simply shut the world out completely. We all have our own way of dealing with it. Not everyone who has been to war, was in combat. Not everyone had to take a life, or see lives taken in front of them. One thing about war is for sure, no one returns unwounded.

THE LAST WAR

You

The waves are crashing over me,
Pulling me ever so down,
I fight and struggle to survive,
But You don't see anything wrong,

You don't see me looking for the danger areas,
Where the enemy will hide,
How I enter the room,
The hazards along the roads,

Faces from the past come back,
The smells,
The voices,
The heat from which there is no escape,

Sleep is no comfort,
Cause I don't really sleep,
I don't want to see this anymore,
And yet I can't get it out of my head,

Who are You to judge me,
You don't know what I have been through,
You don't know how I feel,
And yet You sit there with a smile on your face,

To hell with you,
Your reality is not my reality,
I am trained to show no weakness,
I don't deserve your condescending attitude,

I pray for a little bit of normalcy,
To find a few moments of peace,
Just to catch my breath,
To feel good again,

You say I look fine,
This struggle within you cannot begin to understand,
PTSD is my war,

MICHAEL F. MORTON

War is my reality.

I finished this poem on 24 April 2015. The inspiration for this poem came from watching a news article on PTSD, and the horrible treatment of Veterans with PTSD. YOU CANNOT SEE PTSD!!!!!! But it's there. The treatment of combat veterans and how they are judged is despicable. I am sorry if people find this offensive, but your reality is not theirs. Unless you have been through the horrors yourself, how can you judge what you don't know? You cannot come home from a year or more of death and destruction and just turn it off. You will still be in a hyper vigilant state of alertness. You have been trained to see the danger areas, and you see them. During my combat tours I averaged about 4 hours of sleep a day, but you really don't sleep. When you come home from war, you are exhausted. You sleep, but you really don't get restful sleep for many years. We all try to find peace, to catch our breath from the marathon that is war. Just because we may look normal, doesn't mean there isn't a war raging within.

MICHAEL F. MORTON

My War

>I love to watch the sunsets,
>And listen to the birds on high,
>The laughter of my children,
>But I miss my war
>
>War is exciting,
>A continuous moment in awe,
>Where your senses come alive,
>In a serene state of excitement,
>
>The sounds of war,
>Soldiers laughing,
>The roar of gunfire,
>The silence of the soul,
>
>I am home now, safe,
>But feel foreign,
>Like a stranger in a familiar dream,
>A Deja vu that should not be,
>
>Dreams in horror haunt my mind,
>The images sicken me,
>But their familiarity pulls me in,
>A painful comfort of peace,
>
>Some are memories best forgotten,
>Others I want to remember,
>To live through it again,
>To feel the edge one more time,
>
>But I feel hollow inside,
>As the tremors ever linger,
>Like being in a terrible storm,
>Both powerful and helpless,
>
>I am hungry for it,
>Thirsting for that feeling,
>The edge,

THE LAST WAR

Where control and chaos co-exist,
And yet I hate it,
The death and destruction,
The senseless loss of life,
The rage of violence that was always close,

A place where death is ever present,
And it doesn't really matter,
I miss the high,
I desire the unknown,

Only those who have been,
Know the darkness of war,
The never-ending emptiness,
The thrill that only it can be,

There is no freedom after war,
Only a lonely burden of guilt to carry,
But you crave it,
The death and rebirth of your soul,

The war has twisted my path in life,
Light is dark, dark is light,
For better or worse,
I see the world differently,

I can see the comfort in my family's eyes,
I am home, safe,
Life continues with no uncertainty,
But I miss my war.

I finished this poem on 28 March 2014. The inspiration for this poem came from talking with my fellow comrades of whom we served in combat together. Even though we despise war, we miss it. We don't miss the death and destruction; we miss the high of adrenalin. We miss the bonds made with men you will never forget. We miss living on the edge, in a place where control and chaos exist together. Imagine being a 19-year-old young man, deployed to combat with the power of life or death in your hands. At 19 you are in charge of 6 other young men, and you are responsible for their lives and millions of dollars of worth of military equipment. You spend a year or more training for war, then a year or more at war. The entire time you eat together, you live together, and you fight side by side. You become closer to these men than you are to your families. When you return from a combat tour, many Soldiers leave the military, while some move on to another duty station. You see the world differently, and for better or worse, you will miss it.

Left Behind

I need your help,
So that I can carry on,
To take away the dimness of my soul,
To find the answers,
Of the questions left behind,

This is not something you expect,
Not something you expect for yourself,
Your life is changed forever,
You never get your old self back,

Step by step I try to move forward,
But I am not getting anywhere,
Everything in life has stopped,
So many unknown questions with unknown answers,

You try to get through it,
To get beyond it,
But you never find the solution,
To the why,

I can't ask you to wear my glasses,
If you cannot see my pain,
I can't tell you what it's like to leave this world,
Only what it's like to be left behind,

Leaving life behind is not a favor,
No one is better off without you,
You are not a burden in life,
Please do not leave a burden after life,

If you cannot find a reason to stay someday,
Stay for someone else just for the day,
Then as a gift for someone else, another day,
Then for another, and another, and another,

Don't jump!
My arms are here to hold you,

MICHAEL F. MORTON

My hands are here to guide you,
I will find the answers to the questions, you want to leave behind.

I finished this poem on 5 October 2017

On 4 October 2017, I was notified that a former Soldier of mine, I still consider them mine even though I'm retired, had committed suicide. We served together in combat, and I considered him a true warrior and gentleman. I was in shock, there were no warning signs noted, and now there are only unknown questions with unknown answers. My heart was heavy that day and still is. This is something that continues to happen across the world and it must be stopped.

Suicide is a permeant solution to a temporary problem. I have preached that message for years, and I will go on preaching until everyone hears it. I want to reach as many people as possible that suicide is never an answer. You are not a burden, and no one will ever be better off without you. Leaving behind the world only leaves the burden and pain you could not find the answers to.

PTSD is not an exclusive club to the military and veterans. Many people who have struggled with PTSD have committed suicide. Even more people with PTSD are considering it. We must get them to listen, to believe, that suicide is not the answer to their questions. Suicide will only leave a lifetime of unknown answers to unknown questions for everyone around them.

Please, please, please! I beg you, those that are struggling with thoughts of harming yourself. There is always an answer, always a tomorrow, and always someone who cares for you. Don't be afraid to speak up and ask for help.

To my Brothers and Sisters out there, I and we are here for you. I offer my heart to listen, and my hands to guide you. If you cannot find a reason to stay someday, stay for someone else. Stay as a gift to someone else the next day, and then another and another. Stay and we will help you find the answers to the questions that cannot be left behind.

Always Tomorrow

Where do you go,
When the demons come,
And you think you're lost,
And there is no tomorrow,

You don't give up!
When you don't know where to turn,
Cause I'm standing beside you,
I will help you through,

I will fight your fight,
And never let you go,
No permanent solutions,
To temporary problems will you find,

Brother to Brother,
I will not let you fall,
Nor fight alone,
This war within,

I won't let you go,
No matter how long it takes,
You're going to make it,
You will always have a tomorrow.

I finished this poem on 28 May 2015. This poem is a message to all those who are struggling with PTSD. You are not alone, and you don't have to fight alone. Your brothers and sisters are here for you, no matter how long it takes. You don't give up! You never give up! There is always a tomorrow.

Marine

In the tavern Tun 1775,
They gathered to make their plan,
A Corps of their own,
In freedoms call they'd make their stand,

From across America they came,
To the Island that time forgot,
Or on the beach in Diego Bay,
They marched in suns blazing hot,

The Eagle, Globe and Anchor,
Our coveted symbol we hold true,
Of the very, very proud,
And only a special few,

A sacred brotherhood,
Of once and always we will be,
We fight our countries battles,
In the Air, on Land, and Sea,

From the Halls of Montezuma,
And beyond the boundaries of foreign shores,
We splashed upon the Islands rock,
And crawled along the jungles floors,

Noble is our cause,
In every climb and place,
First to fight are the hounds of hell,
Our destiny we gladly face,

Across the Seven Seas,
If the world ever looks on heaven's scene,
They will find us always faithful,
And our title always Marine.

I finished this poem on 10 November 2014, the 239th birthday of the United States Marine Corps. I started my military career in the Marine Corps, and served with some of the greatest men I have ever known. So this poem is for you Devil Dogs, Leather Necks, Semper Fi.

Changed

I am back in the world now,
Everyone says I have changed,

I don't feel different,
But I see everything differently,

I don't sweat the small stuff any longer,
Life's priorities have changed,

Everyone wants to talk to me,
How can I explain war,
The comradeship,
The death and destruction,
The anger of loss I carry,

I feel better when I am alone with my thoughts,
No one would understand them anyway,

I am called a Vet now,
But I don't know what that means,

The old Vets give me a nod and a smile,
But it brings no comfort,

Have I changed,
Or am I lost in time,

I don't see flags flying any longer,
I guess they have forgotten,

But I cannot forget,
I carry the memories of those brothers whom I served,
And long to be back in the fight,

I guess I have changed,
But I don't really care.

THE LAST WAR

I finished this poem on 6 March 2013. This poem is about what it's like to return home from war. Back to the world, home in the U.S., and when you get home, you won't be the same you. You won't feel any different, but you will see things differently. Things that used to bother you, you will shrug off as no big deal. Everyone will want to talk to you, asking you questions you never want to hear. "did you kill anyone?", "did you see any dead bodies?", "what's it really like in war?". How do you explain something no one will understand? Unless they have been there, and trust me, if they've been there, they won't ask.

Back home you are called a Vet, but what does the mean. You see the Vets at the VA, but that brings no comfort, you still feel alone. All the flags that were flying when you left are gone. What we call patriotism on the fly, only when it's convenient and then they forget. They have forgotten something you never will. You will come to learn that you have changed, you are different, but you don't really care.

Etched in Stone

We are alive,
We live to tell their tales,
Tales of the ones we once knew,
Whose names are etched in stone,

They came when duty did call,
Summoned by the cause,
To defend freedom,
To keep hope alive,

Their scars we carry,
The scars of things seen and done,
We carry them with pride,
We carry them with guilt and shame,

Our souls are wounded,
Never to be made whole,
With silent hopes and dreams,
Of those left behind,

They battled and charged,
And now move no more,
Not knowing their victory,
Over the lingering mist of death,

Now free of struggle and pain,
The price paid in full,
Our hearts still hold true,
Their memory we live eternal,

We never need reminded,
We remember those we called brother,
As their names are etched in stone,
And in our hearts forever.

This poem was finished on 11 July 2014. This poem is about remembrance, remembering the names of the fallen. When you return from war, you are changed forever. Ingrained with experiences you will never forget, especially the loss of a brother or sister. You learn to deal with grief in your own fashion. But you are never prepared to see the name of your brother or sister engraved into a tombstone. That's when you must come to terms this is permanent.
Just as their names are engraved into the stone, so it is in your heart. You remember all the things you did together, and carry those scars "memories" everywhere you go. Scars will fade with time, but these memories never go away. You will never forget your brothers and sisters' names, as they are etched in your heart forever.

MICHAEL F. MORTON

My Brothers Mine

My Brothers' Mine,
I honor your name,
Your bravery and valor,
I remember you,

We fought together,
In the fires of hell,
From which there is no escape,
The cost of life, your life,

Precious is life,
That we take for granted,
We risk it not blindly,
But for those in life we entrust,

The blood of battle forever stains,
The blood of battle forever bonds,
Our brothers' memories we keep,
Our bonds we hold sacred,

This bond we share,
We are humbled to follow,
Hopeful to live up to,
And honored to share with those like us,

To those who have passed the sight of man,
This we do pledge,
Those that follow will keep the faith,
They will keep our memory,

My Brothers' Mine,
Our blood the same blood,
I honor your spirit,
I honor your name.

This poem was finished on 27 May 2014. This poem is about the bonds forged in combat. When you fight in war, you don't fight for the cause, you fight for the brothers to your left and right. This bond is hard to explain if you have never served in combat. Not that all bonds made in the service aren't special, but these bonds are forever. Even as the years pass, or some have passed away, they are my brothers, and I am theirs. Alpha Company, 1st Battalion, 6th Infantry Regiment. Raiders For Life!

The Cell

I live in this cell,
Deep in the dark,
Afraid of the light,
All alone,

Built by my own hands,
I come here every day,
My place of refuge,
My living hell,

I want to forget,
But try to relive it,
Again and again,
Each and every day,

I shut the world out,
Even the ones that love me,
It's not on purpose,
Why, I can't understand,

I try to venture out,
To be part of the world,
Only to find myself,
Longing to be back in my cell,

I'm so tired,
Sleep is never enough,
Always in a haze,
Never finding my clarity,

When will the light come in,
When will I be found,
When will this end,
When will I let it?

This poem was finished on 10 April 2013. This poem is about living with PTSD and not knowing it. For some, PTSD is like living in a cell, a cell that you create. You become reclusive, withdrawn from everyone. You go to your cell because that's where you feel safe. You try to venture out, to find that peace you used to know. But all you can think about is going back to your cell. You don't understand why this is happening, you cannot explain how you feel. Why you are shutting everyone out. You feel like you're in a fog, nothing is clear. In this state of PTSD all you want to do is sleep, but you don't sleep enough not matter how long you stay in bed.

Our combat tours in Iraq and Afghanistan were usually a year, some 13 to 15 months long. Your train up for deployment is about a year, with a training tempo that is like a combat schedule. When you finally make it home, you haven't really slept for about two years. Combat is not a 9-5 schedule, operations continue around the clock. An average day for us was about 18 hours. There were times when you would choose sleep over eating, and you kept this up for a year or more. When you come home you think you will sleep soundly, NOPE! You have been hypervigilant for a year, you can't just shut it off. Now add the struggle of PTSD, and you never know when it's going to hit you. When you are in your cell, you want the light to come in. you just don't know how to do it. It may sound simple to you, but getting out isn't easy. It takes time and support from those you love and trust. You must let the light come in, in order to get out.

The Dance

It's the first night out in the dance,
The music is playing,
our boots are on tight,
I wonder how the dance will be,

I can feel the ground shaking,
thunder pounding in my ears as the dance begins,
Red and green fire flies fill the night air,
dancing around me like fireworks on the fourth of July,

I step into the lead,
as it's my turn to join the dance,
Rushing winds zip by my head with startling speed,
The fire flies swarm around me,
moving ever closer with the music,

The music is changing;
deafening screams pierce the intensity,
thunder and lightning are everywhere,
Angry birds flying overhead are joining the dance,
The music from their wings,
overpower the night,

Time seams an eternity,
the music now silent,
The dance is over, the skies are clear,
My heart and mind still racing,
It was my first night at the dance,
only 454 days more to go.

I finished this poem on 14 January 2013. This poem is about my first combat mission in Sadr City, Iraq. I was on my third combat tour to Iraq, and serving as the First Sergeant of Company A, 1st Battalion, 6th Infantry Regiment, 3rd Brigade Combat Team, 1st Armored Division, Baumholder Germany. I know that's a mouthful, but I honor those whom I served with, and they deserve to be recognized.

Our mission in Sadr City was to build a sixteen-foot-high, four-kilometer wall down the middle of the enemy stronghold. The concept for building the wall was to keep the insurgents out of the area, so they couldn't shoot rockets and mortars into the middle of Baghdad. The rocket and mortar attacks were killing hundreds of people and had to be stopped.

We headed out at about 6pm for a 12-hour mission. Yes, I said 12 hours. The music playing is a reference to the sounds of combat. Everything from the sound of vehicle engines to the explosions of rockets impacting around you. The moment we stepped foot on the ground, we were attacked from multiple directions. Combat in an urban area is always a 360-degree fight, there are no front lines, no safe zones. Mortar rounds started impacting around us, the enemy tracers (bullets) filled the air. The tanks and Bradley Fighting Vehicles were firing their main guns, and we were engaging the enemy with our rifles. The sounds of bullets rushing by your head, there was no mistake, we were in the fight of our lives.

As the battle continues, you hear a Soldier scream "Medic", and others yelling out orders to move and shoot the enemy. The Apache helicopters join the fight, shooting their 25mm cannon and Hellfire missiles at the enemy. Buildings are exploding and collapsing along the street, as smoke fills the air like a grey veil. Even with your combat earplugs in, its deafening.

When the battle ends, you have no reference of time. We were in the fight for about 3 hours, but it seemed like days. My heart didn't stop racing for about another hour as we regrouped and re-armed all our weapons. I couldn't help but think about the fight we were just in, and this was just the first day. How are we going to keep this up for 15 months?

The Day

In plywood coffins,
Their fate began,
Across the sea,
To waiting sand,

Hell on earth,
They met face to face,
Quick to cover,
But found no place,

A sea of red,
And hails of fire,
Through, metal, earth, and bodies dead,
Their efforts did not tire,

They clung together,
Arm and hand,
In the face of death,
Their brothers band,

On that day,
The greatest generation did prove,
Tyranny will end,
And oppressors removed,

The fate of the world,
Did rest on a prayer,
On a June summer morn,
The burden they did bear.

This poem was finished on 6 June 2013, the 69th anniversary of D-Day during World War II. The landing boats that carried the troops ashore were made of plywood, which means the enemy bullets would go right through it. It is estimated that over 450,000 Allied and German troops were killed or wounded during the allied invasion of Europe. When they hit the beaches, there was no cover, no place to hide. They had to fight their way forward or the would die. The sea was red with blood, and bodies were scattered everywhere. Despite all the horrors faced that day, they kept fighting. The greatest generation paid the price of freedom for the world. They deserve our respect, and shall be remembered forever.

The Garden

A special stone,
In the Garden grows,
Side by side,
They stand in rows,

Sacred ground,
Where valor proudly sleeps,
The Soldiers gather,
And family weeps,

A reverent memorial,
An image to behold,
Bears whiteness to the sacrifice,
Of those few told,

Their sun has set,
Their shadows tell the tale,
A hero has come home,
The guns do hail,

Listen to the Silence,
The message loud and clear,
Honor and freedom,
Our Nation holds dear,

The bugle cries,
Farewells are shown,
There is silence in the garden,
Another stone has grown.

I finished this poem on 20 March 2013. This poem is about Arlington National Cemetery, and the military funerals I have seen. If you have never been there, it is a very humbling experience. The burial grounds are called "The Garden", and the grave markers "Stones". Unfortunately, I have been to too many memorial services, both as a guest and as part of the Honor Guard. Every time the guns fire the 21 Gun Salute, you jump; every time you hear Taps, your heart sinks. The Stones stand in formation as far as you can see, and the garden grows every day.

The Fix

                The Fix,
          Waiting for the fight,
       The thrilling dance with death,
       The walk upon no man's land,

                The Fix,
A place where life is multiplied by infinity,
The constant awareness of one's own mortality,
      A total focus in the moment,

                The Fix,
              The smell,
         The air bitter sweet,
The sounds only one who's been there knows,

                The Fix,
    Alive above and beyond normal life,
   A compulsive craving for uncertainty,
       The usual of the unusual,

                The Fix,
The dirty little secret that no one talks about,
       The feeling of unfeeling,
    The broad numbness of all feeling,

        I've tried to find it,
    The euphoric rush of aliveness,
  The thrill of looking death in the eye,
    And the laughter when he blinks,

No excitement now can fill my void,
My thirst for life goes unquenched,
The terror filled thrill of survival,
         The Fix.

THE LAST WAR

I finished this poem on 7 September 2017. This poem is about combat and missing the complete adrenalin rush from being there. If you've been to combat, you hate combat. When you get out of the military, you will miss it. You don't miss the death and destruction, you miss the time when you were most alive. You miss the sounds, the feel of a weapon in your hands. In combat you are alive in every moment, for every moment may be your last. You crave the unknown, and the unknown of each day becomes the usual. You are there with your Brothers, and it's the best time of your life. When you get out of the military, you try to replace the adrenalin fix; but it's just not the same. So, your thirst goes unquenched, and the fix unfilled.

Blood on Blood

You Don't call us Brother,
Unless we are Brothers,
Our Brotherhood is greater than any association,
It is the very price of our survival,

You cannot contribute to our ideal,
To the heart of our Brotherhood,
No matter how much you preach it,
Unless you've lived it,

It matters not where we come from,
Our oath is powerful and strong,
We fight as one,
We are a force with a courageous path,

Our Brotherhood has no color or creed,
As our spirit needs no publicity,
We walk a journey without end,
And carry the mark of war,

Our strength comes from our principles,
As we stand as one in the face of adversity,
Brothers stand with Brothers,
And Brothers don't let Brothers walk alone in the dark,

Our destiny has made us Brothers,
No one goes their own way,
All that we give for the lives of others,
Will come back to our own,

Blood on Blood,
Brothers stronger than blood,
I may not be my brother's keeper,
But I am my Brother's Brother.

This poem was written on 15 June 2017. This may be hard for some to hear, but you don't call us brother unless we are brothers. Brother is a term that is thrown around very loosely these days, and I'm not saying it isn't used sincerely. In the military, we don't call each other brother, unless we have earned that title. You cannot talk the talk, unless you've lived it.

I have served with some great people in my military career. Some are acquaintances, some are comrades, and few are called Brother. If you are called brother, you are a brother for life. We are not our brother's keeper, but we are our brothers brother.

Our brotherhood has no borders, colors, or creeds, and we see no need to publicize it to the world. We will always stand together, no matter the years and miles between us. Brothers stand with Brothers, and brothers never say goodbye.

Ease My Storm

The Storms are raging,
Waves are crashing against the shattered soul,
The world is drowning,
In a place where peace has no name,

The mighty winds begin to rise,
As the thunder roars its silent fury,
The skies are ill and decaying,
Leaving broken shards of life upon the shore,

I am the Hunter,
At war with my nature,
Searching for a sign of hope,
Traveling the distance to nowhere and everywhere,

Engulfed by a hardened black consciousness,
The solitary of my existence has sought without knowing,
For the sins I must atone,
Memories only serve to fuel the fire,

My greatest fear,
To wander an eternity,
A mind ever searching,
A mind turned unenergetic and complacent,

Can this soul be rescued,
Will this mind find its peace,
Can this heart that beats within be salvaged,
For my body and soul can run no more,

I seek the light,
No longer the fire,
To feel the gentle rain,
And find the peace to ease my storm.

This poem was written on 2 May 2017. This poem is about PTSD. There are many forms of PTSD, and it depends on the person how they experience it. Some people will experience many different forms of PTSD at the same time, ever changing as they go through their journey.

This poem is about being in a storm, the waves (emotions) are crashing down on you. You try to rise about it, and another wave crashes over you. Your life becomes shattered visions, memories of life scattered across an unclear mind. Part of you remembers the hunter, the warrior you are, while another part is searching for its identity.

You seclude yourself away from everyone, fighting the darkness and yet you enjoy its embrace. Left alone with your memories, they drive you to your greatest fears, being alone. You scream "save me" as loud as you can, but it's only inside your head, because you dare not make a sound and reveal your weakness.

Whatever form of PTSD someone has, we all tend to have the same desire, to find our peace. Just to feel good again, without having to chemically enhance ourselves to get there.

For me the road to peace came from one my own leadership philosophies called "Small Victories". Instead of trying to immerse myself into things, I started with something simple, like bubble baths. I know that may sound weird, but it helped calm my mind, helped me relax. Pretty soon I looked forward to them, then I was ready to try something else, then another and another.

I cannot tell you what your small victories are; only you can discover them. The theory works, I have used it for years, and it has helped me overcome many obstacles in life. I hope this will help you in some way too.

Left Behind

I need your help,
So that I can carry on,
To take away the dimness of my soul,
To find the answers,
Of the questions left behind,

This is not something you expect,
Not something you expect for yourself,
Your life is changed forever,
You never get your old self back,

Step by step I try to move forward,
But I am not getting anywhere,
Everything in life has stopped,
So many unknown questions with unknown answers,

You try to get through it,
To get beyond it,
But you never find the solution,
To the why,

I can't ask you to wear my glasses,
If you cannot see my pain,
I can't tell you what it's like to leave this world,
Only what it's like to be left behind,

Leaving life behind is not a favor,
No one is better off without you,
You are not a burden in life,
Please do not leave a burden after life,

If you cannot find a reason to stay someday,
Stay for someone else just for the day,
Then as a gift for someone else, another day,
Then for another, and another, and another,

Don't jump!

THE LAST WAR

My arms are here to hold you,
My hands are here to guide you,
I will find the answers to the questions, you want to leave behind.

This poem was written on 3 October 2017. This poem is about a serious tragedy that takes an average of 22 veterans' lives every day, suicide. This poem is also very personal, and I wrote it the day that one of my former Solders committed suicide. Suicide is heartbreaking no matter who it is, and the questions left behind never get answered. When I heard the news about my Soldier, I still refer to all the Soldiers I served with as mine, I was shocked and dumbfounded. I couldn't believe it, it just couldn't be true. How could this happen, we all keep in touch through social media, we are committed to a brotherhood that will always be. Why? I asked myself. Why does this keep happening?

One of the goals of my writing is to reach those who may be hurting. To let them know there is always someone is there, someone who will listen, who won't judge, someone who will never leave them behind. Hopefully reach them

To those that may be hurting, let me tell you from my heart, the world is not better off without you. You are not doing anyone a favor, you are not a burden, so please don't leave the burden of why behind. Please understand, when people leave this life, there is still life left behind. And the life left behind is now changed forever. There are so many unknown questions, "why", that will never be answered. Why will be the question and burden that will last their lifetime.

I cannot tell you what's on the other side, but I can tell you what it's like to be left behind. I have lost too many over that last 10 years to this tragedy, and I am still hurting, still trying to understand why. It's not just me that's hurting, its everyone that knew them, and the family members of those that knew them. That's right, my children see the hurt, they see the pain and it gets to them, and they never met my brothers that are now gone.

Please, please, please listen. If you are hurting out there, and you cannot find a reason to stay for another day. Stay for me, stay for someone else another day. Then as a gift, stay for someone else another day. Then for another, and another, and another. Then do it all over again. I know you can do it!!!

We all need to help one another, help find the answers to the question why, before why becomes a reality.

No Escape

> The city falls silent,
> as the sun fades from view,
>
> A wall of brown sweeps down upon us,
> Covering the earth like a dirty blanket,
>
> The air is impenetrable,
> blinding all that see,
>
> Sand fills your lungs,
> from which there is no escape,
>
> Nothing moves,
> as if the city has stopped in time,
>
> The only sound our enemies attack,
> using the wall to obscure their evil deeds,
>
> My war is long since over,
> but the brown blanket still covers me,
>
> Try as I might,
> it cannot be removed,
> The sand still fills my lungs,
> from which there is no escape.

This poem was written on 4 February 2013. This poem is about the sand storms we had to survive in Iraq, called "Haboobs". Some of these sand storms are so high and so wide they engulf entire cities, with winds blowing as high as 50 mph. when they hit, there is no escape. There is no place you can go that the sand will not get through. You cannot see, it's almost impossible to breath, and if you don't cover your face, it will feel like you are being sandblasted.

When the Haboob hits, nothing moves, nothing except the enemy. It was their tactic to go out in this nightmare, plant the IED's (roadside bombs), and wait for us to come by. Many times we were out on patrol missions when the storms would hit, you either stopped and waited, or tried to drive back to your combat outpost. Depending on where and when you were in Iraq, would depend on what you would do. The only constant about these storms, you knew the enemy was going to attack. Every storm we encountered, we were attacked multiple times, and there were always IED strikes. If there was an IED strike close to your combat outpost, you would get in your vehicles and go help those that were hit.

When the storm is finally over, sand is everywhere. All over you, inside everything and in places you never thought the sand could be. It leaves an orange tint to your skin that was exposed, and you feel like you are breathing with a gas mask on. Many years after the war, I still feel it hard to breath. Like there is still sand in my lungs. So if you ever wondered why so many veterans have respiratory issues, this is probably one of the main causes.

Tags of Silver

> They are never correct,
> the first time you get them,
>
> They are never comfortable to wear,
> but you wear them,
>
> They make a special sound,
> that only they can make,
>
> If you lose them,
> it's no big deal,
> you just go get more,
>
> When they hang from an inverted rifle,
> with your brother's name on them,
> they mean the world to you.

This poem was written on 4 February 2013. This poem is about a Soldiers Identification Tags, more commonly known as dog tags.

When you get your first set of "Dog Tags" there are usually errors. Your name miss spelled, wrong blood type, wrong religion. And sometimes it will take months for them to be made correctly. Why, who knows?

You think they are cool at first, but not comfortable at all to wear. They make a special sound that only they can make, and if you hear it, you know exactly what it is. If you lose them, and you will, it's no big deal, just ask for more, and the whole process starts over again. In truth, they are no big deal and most Soldiers don't really wear them.

When a Soldier dies in combat, a memorial service is held and what's known as a Soldiers Cross or Battlefield Cross is placed at the front of the chapel. This cross consists of the Soldiers boots at the base, a rifle inverted, the Soldiers helmet at the top. Hanging from the rifle pistol grip is the fallen Soldiers Dog Tags.

Like I mentioned before, most guys don't wear their dog tags or care if they lose them. When they are hanging from an inverted rifle with your brother's name on them, it means the world to you. That's when the reality hits you, they are gone

THE LAST WAR

Retrieved from Army memorial service that I attended for one on my Soldiers in 2008.

The Helmet and Identification tags signify the fallen Soldier, their name never to be forgotten. The inverted rifle with bayonet signals a time for prayer, a break in the battle to pay tribute to our brother or sister. The worn combat boots represent the final march, of the Soldiers last battle.

MICHAEL F. MORTON

Silence In My Foxhole

Demoralized I sit in my hole,
I see the world around me,
Even in the light, it is dark, cold and silent,

I try to remember happy thoughts,
the faces and laughter of times past,

The world starts to close in around me.
I am in the company of my comrades,
the chaos of war raining down upon us,

My eyes only see fire,
The deafening screams fill my ears,
until they are no more, silent,

The fire and smoke are gone now,
The screams of war have ended,
The silence I hear is not in my ears,
but in my heart,

My brothers will cry no more.
There is nothing but silence in my foxhole.

This poem was written on 14 January 2013. This poem is about PTSD and having nightmares about traumatic experiences in combat. The foxhole is your "safe zone", the place where you feel safe. Most people suffering from PTSD will have a safe zone, and they will instinctively go there when they are stressed.

Even though it's your safe zone, you will still suffer from stress and nightmares. You try to surround yourself with positive things, but the nightmares can penetrate your armor. Some of the worst nightmares involve being back in the war, reliving the trauma. You see the fire, you feel the heat, you hear the cries of the dying. Until the nightmare ends, and you awake.

Silence in the foxhole, is not a silence of the ears, but a silence in the heart. You are left with the reality that your brothers or sisters are gone. And you retreat even more into the foxhole, only to relive the nightmare again and again.

MICHAEL F. MORTON

The Final Lullaby

My day is done,
the faint echo of a lullaby,
resounding in my mind,

The melody fills my heart,
as I prepare my body to drift a slumber.

I cannot turn it off,
this lullaby,
triggers my mind to reflect the day's events,

The gathering in honor,
with heads held heavy,
anticipating the final bugle call,

The lullaby;
a song of peace, sorrow, and rest.

This final lullaby, life is no more.

The world stands rigid,
honors rendered by all hands.

The music stirs our soul,
until the lullaby cries no more.

This poem was written on 18 January 2013. This poem is about the military bugle song called "Taps". In the early days of the Army, they used bugle calls to signal messages to the troops. There were bugle calls to wake you up "Reveille", bugle calls to signal the end of the day "Retreat" and one signal the last call of the day, bedtime, "Taps".

The origin of Taps varies, but the common accepted history of the song is of a lullaby. Played at the end of the day to signal the troops it was time to rest. The song now is played on military installations at 11 PM, and at the end of military funerals.

When I was a young Soldier stationed in Germany, you would hear the bugle call played, and often we would joke that its bedtime, the party was over. The first time I heard Taps at a military funeral, I felt my heart drop, and the reality of the situation hit me life a ton of bricks. After that, the song took on a new meaning.

When my first Soldier was killed in combat, I wasn't ready for the memorial service. I did my best to be strong and lead from the front, but when Taps played, I could not hold back the tears. The realization that my Soldier was gone, and this was the final lullaby, our final goodbye. I will always remember that song and the loss associated with it.

If you have never heard the bugle call "Taps", take a minute and listen, I think you will understand how powerful the song truly is.

What It Takes

What do you think it takes to fight?
What kind of person do you think I am?
The life I live isn't pretty or kind.

My blood is red like yours,
But I breath Red, White, and Blue.

The truth is you are afraid of me,
But you need me when its time,
When the wolf is at the door,
And until then you discard me,
Turn a deaf ear when I return from killing the wolf.

I wasn't born this way
I learned what it takes to fight,
To survive the wolf,

The warrior spirit burns in me,
Begging to be released,
Yet praying I don't have too,

You don't know what it takes,
What I have seen,
What I have lived,
We fight so you can believe your lies.

Take a look inside,
See if you could have endured all that we have,
And still never give up on you.

THE LAST WAR

This poem was written on 31 October 2012. The inspiration for this poem comes from hearing certain politicians talk about the military. I will make the disclaimer that not all politicians or people in general are negative about the military, but in this case, this person stated that people in the military were unintelligent, over paid and not cost effective to America. I wish I could have had a chance to respond to his comments, but it was televised.

I will let the poem speak for its self, but I will add this; if you have never served, how can you talk about what you know nothing about? I could easily go on a rant, vent my anger and frustrations about their comments. But I will just leave it at this, "You're Welcome"!

Painless

The pain I live with burns deep inside.
I dare not speak of it,
for I know not its meaning.

I try to quiet my pain,
with numbing senseless.

The more I hide my pain,
the more it breeds inside me.

I dare not show it to those closest to me,
for I cannot explain my pain.
No solutions I see.

I am painless now;
I have passed it on to you.
It was not intended so,
it was my unconscious solution.

I bid farewell my brothers.
Speak not my tale in gathered silence.

Share my story with brothers and sisters alike.
It must be told to stop others in such pain,
for being painless is no solution.

This poem was written on 17 January 2013. This poem is about PTSD, the struggles of living with PTSD, and unfortunately how it sometimes ends up. People struggling with PTSD don't talk about it, they are afraid to talk about it, because they don't understand it themselves and believe no one else will. Instead, they try to numb the pain with alcohol, drugs, and dangerous adrenalin rush activities. All of these activities prove to make their situation worse.

Many people with PTSD tend push everyone away, even those closest to them. They are consumed by their pain, and see no way out. This tends to lead to excessive numbing and sometimes suicide. Suicide, the permanent solution, to temporary problems.

It's very hard to say goodbye to a brother or sister you served with. It's even harder with someone who has committed suicide. In my experiences, I and everyone else didn't see it coming. We were left with the question "why", and their pain has now become our burden to carry.

This is something we need to talk about my brothers and sisters. We need to share with each other, so this doesn't happen again. It is not a sign of weakness to get help, and there are people who will understand. I did it, and so can you. I know it's hard, I know it's a struggle, but being painless is not a solution.

Left And Right

To the Left and Right,
Is where I long to be,
Where everything made sense,
Where I know I belong,

To the Left and Right,
A kinship evolves,
A kinship in cause,
Rising out of great need,

To the Left and Right,
We fought as one,
For reasons unspoken,
The tragedies only we can know,

No statues or symbols,
Fueled the drive within our fight,
For those who did courageous things,
Were found upon our Left and Right,

To the Left and Right,
We are not lost to forgotten years,
And though we may pass from the sight of man,
Our promise imbued by honor,

To the Left and Right,
A life we chose to live,
A life that shall never rest,
Until victory is ours,

To the Left and Right,
With my Brothers I long to be,
Where everything makes sense,
Where I know I belong.

THE LAST WAR

This poem was written on 1 August 2016. This poem is about the bonds and brotherhood established in war.

To the left and right, our brothers and sisters train and fight by our side. We don't do it for money, medals or parades; we simply do it for each other. We fight as one, we endure the tragedies together. Everyone's combat tours are different, we don't fight the same fights, and we don't experience the same horrors. What we do endure creates a bond that last a lifetime.

You want to know why we fight. The answer is simple. We don't fight for you; we don't fight for honor or glory. We fight in combat for the brother or sister to our left and right. We serve our country for you; we serve our country to defend its honor, to protect our way of life. When it comes down to it, it's the person to our left and right that's got our back. They are there in the middle of the fire next to you, and you trust them with your life. How many people do you share that kind of trust with? The kind of trust you don't have to talk about, you don't have to think about, because you know it's there, and they do as well.

I am retired from the Army now, but I miss those days immensely. I don't miss the death and destruction of war, or being away from home for a year or more. I miss the comradery, I miss the honor among men. I miss my brothers to the left and right.

The Nobel Warrior

The Nobel Warrior,
Whose battles fought far and wide,
Days now pass with darkened sky,
His will fleeting, as the fire slowly dies,

Living in the service of others,
But always alone,
Contesting the struggle for order,
With victory life, with failure death,

Through weary eyes,
He can still see the flame,
Still hear the wolf,
Ever present at the door,

Enraptured by the terrors of battles missed,
He fears the fight is gone,
Uncertainty has cloaked his mind,
His release only a breath away,

Unheeded by his tribe,
The foolish and fearful see with blinded eye,
No longer seen the champion,
His prowess and valor forgotten,

Never a battle lost or won,
Time hath not eclipsed,
Nor death discouraged,
His whisper for peace,

The Nobel Warrior,
Whose days now pass with darkened sky,
The battlefields now empty,
His shield and sword resigned.

This poem was written on 12 December 2016. The inspiration for this poem came from watching a war movie. The main character, the top warrior, always there for his Soldiers, but rarely home. They are abandoned by family, who cannot see their dedication to protect them at all costs. That may sound farfetched, but I can tell you that is a pretty accurate description of most career warriors.

These noble warriors dedicate their life to serving others, but are always alone. Even with family and friends around them, they are alone. As they are always on guard, always ready to fight the wolf at the door. They endeavor to find order in life, with victory there is life, with failure is death.

The greatest fear of any warrior is the fear of no longer being considered dangerous. The fear that the fight inside is gone, and doubt has taken hold in their life. They remember the fight, the sounds, and the smells. Always prepared for war, but praying it never comes.

Always Possible

I cannot see the storms in your eyes,
I cannot hear the silence in your heart,
I cannot know the recklessness in your soul,
Unless you let me,

My heavy heart does not bear a humble tongue,
So I ask for no forgiveness,
These chains that have weighed you down,
Can always be removed,

Open your eyes,
Let us see your despair,
I will take you somewhere safe,
Where the light will fill your heart,

Free yourself,
With the power of forgiveness and humility,
Forgiveness in yourself,
And the humility to take your brothers hand,

Love yourself,
As your brothers love you,
Let us be your hope,
And our bond be your refuge,

There is power in your tears,
They are not a sign of weakness,
You only deepen the wound,
When you neglect to see them,

It's always possible,
When your future seems hazed,
Cling to your brothers,
And we will find your path to peace.

THE LAST WAR

This poem was written on 7 October 2017. This poem is about suffering with PTSD and not asking for help, even from the brothers and sisters they served with. Its always possible when we fight together.

I will no longer be silent, I don't care how many feelings it hurts. PTSD is not a silent code, and we all need to talk about it.

You don't have to suffer in silence, but I cannot help you if you don't let me see. You must let those whom you love, love you back. Asking for help is not a sign of weakness, but a feat of strength and bravery. It's always possible, there will always be a tomorrow. When we fight together, we will all find our peace.

Never Say Goodbye

> Brothers Never Say Goodbye,
> For goodbyes mean going away,
> Going away means forgetting,
> And Brothers never forget Brothers,
>
> Brothers bid farewell,
> A promise of a new future,
> So many goodbyes have been said this year,
> With farewell, no parting is possible,
>
> Saying farewell to our brother,
> Is a most difficult experience in life,
> But we must remember to share in his memory,
> For when the sorrow fades, it is our memories that keep him alive,
>
> Our farewell is not the end,
> For we must lean forward to the next venture beneath the skies,
> We must be the memory that holds his spirit together,
> As we must be the spirit of his memories yet to come,
>
> No distance,
> Or lapse of time,
> Shall lesson the worth,
> Of our brothers recall,
>
> Such as the resiliency of the human heart,
> We must continue to fight forward,
> As he is still by our side,
> The force that drives the sword within our hands,
>
> It is not the ending that haunts us,
> But the space in life where they should be,
> The memories we keep within our hearts,
> Ensure their memories will not fade,
>
> The hardest farewells,
> Are the ones never said,

THE LAST WAR

The ones never explained,
The ones where the story wasn't over,

Those we encounter in life can change us,
And only we can decide the fate of that change,
Because I know you are my brother,
I have been changed for good,

I grieve in the farewell of my brother,
For he is my brother,
And my grief is testimony,
That my brother is so loved I must express it,

As painful as our farewell shall be,
I know we will meet again one day,
For it is certain that those who are brothers,
Shall gather again in Valhalla on high.

This poem was written on 13 November 2017. This poem is very personal, as I wrote it in tribute to a warrior I served with who has passed away from health issues. Our brother Jason passed away on 11 November 2017, Veterans Day.

We are brothers, and because we are brothers, I share my grief as a testimony to love we have for him. I will let the poem speak as the tribute to him. Farewell Jason, my friend, my brother.

Sidelines

So you think you're on the sidelines,
Watching all that is life go by,
Placed there by your unique challenges,
Confined only by your consciousness,

You think you've lost everything,
But you have so much more,
In your heart lies the spark,
In your soul burns the will,

Your challenges are a gift,
A gift that makes you strong enough to overcome it,
Smart enough to figure it out,
And brave enough to use it,

You can endure overwhelming obstacles,
If your belief becomes your conviction,
Obstacles are placed in our paths not to stop us,
But to ignite our strength and courage,

Don't confine your spirit,
Even if you only do one thing well,
You are needed by others,
More than you know,

The journey starts with one belief,
By doing what is necessary,
By doing what is possible,
And soon you are doing the impossible,

The human spirit is one of ability,
Resiliency and courage that no challenge can steal away,
Face the Sunshine,
And your shadows will fall behind.

This poem was written on 25 May 2017. This poem came about after talking with some disabled veterans and hearing some make excuses for getting out and participating in life. I am not saying disabilities are not challenging, but they can truly be a gift if you truly look within.

I have disabilities from my injuries in the war. Mine are not as bad as others, and I don't let them keep me on the sidelines like some with lesser injuries.

When I was wounded the first time in Iraq, three others were also wounded. One of my Soldiers lost both his legs, due to burns from the roadside bomb explosion. Despite his loss, he was the most positive and spirited Solider I have ever known. He didn't let the challenges stop him, and traveled around the hospital motivating everyone around him. After I heard that, I stopped wallowing in depression and decided to get back into the game.

Your challenges are a gift, they can ignite your strengths and stimulate your creativity. All you need is one belief, and soon you will believe anything is possible.

Don't confine your spirit, face your sunshine, and soon your shadows will fall away.

Ghosts Of War

My heart starts pounding,
As I try to push everything into the past,
But the darkness always finds me,
And the darkness always leaves me empty,

Ghosts of war,
For those that live this reality,
Sleep is but a black hole,
Lost for all time,

Living at the mercy of your dreams,
The unsettled particles of a trampled past,
Terrified of all the sensations coming in,
And images going out,

Slipping between the shadows and the light,
They find their way in,
They spring from deep within,
Whispering your deepest fears that cannot be spoken,

Living a nightmare in the darkness of your soul,
They make their exits and entrances as they please,
Even in the day light,
They leave their moldering fingerprints across your day,

The Ghosts of war,
They hold you in their clutches,
Until you,
You decide it's time to let go,

The pain of war,
Will never exceed the anguish of its aftermath,
Only when you decide to stop hiding from the truth,
Will you being to heal

This poem was written on 7 November 2017. This poem is about the nightmares associated with PTSD. Let me make this disclaimer up front, there are all kinds of PTSD, and everyone has their own demons to deal with. Not everyone has the same symptoms or struggles to deal with.

One of the common struggles with PTSD is nightmares. Reliving the traumatic incidents over and over again. Living at the mercy of your dreams, the ghosts (nightmares) find their way in no matter what you do. The effects of these ghosts can even follow you into the daylight, impacting your daily life.

There are ways to conquer these ghosts, but only you can do it for yourself. Seeking help and counseling can give you guidance, but you have to face your truth.

I had to learn to make peace with my ghosts, and let go of the anger I had held deep within for so long. Once I could do that, the ghosts were no more.

THE LAST WAR

The Truth

Truth is the first victim of war,
For war is the violence forever waged against truth,
Every war launched in time,
Is a theft of life for all time,

Those that have seen the truth,
Welcome the light,
For the pain of war,
Will never surpass the aftermath of sorrow,

Everything in war is barbaric,
Forcing man to live like beasts,
To collectively commit acts like beasts,
Deeds which revolt their total being,

This disgrace to mankind,
Must be erased for all time,
Killing under the cloak of war,
Is only a stage of death and pain,

The real distinction of man,
Rest in the victories of peace, never those of war,
For peace demands the fidelity of truth,
And a heroism in peace is far greater than war,

Our world is full of pain and death,
Without the multiplications of war,
We can never create a blueprint for a peaceful tomorrow,
Without creating a tomorrow prepared for war,

To establishing a lasting peace,
We must improve the minds of all mankind,
For there can be no war,
That will end all war.

This poem was written on 3 October 2017. This poem is about truth. As in the truth of war, with truth being the first victim of war. There is no honor or glory in war. Only people who do honorable and glorious things to save their brothers and sisters. There will never be a war that will end war. Read the poem again, look at the words. I hope you will understand.

Haze

>My world has become a dream,
>An alluring nightmare,
>Where life has no reality,
>Encased in the shell of a life long ago,
>
>My senses complicate the minute,
>Turning trifles into tragedies,
>Passions into battles,
>And memories into stormy paths,
>
>I am in a maze that leads nowhere,
>Today and tomorrow race across my mind,
>One day forgets,
>One day waits to arrive,
>
>Doing is painful,
>In a haze of existing without living,
>I am unable to hear, to speak, to breath,
>Swept into the deepest embrace of shadows,
>
>On my darkest days,
>I am safe within my haze,
>With no present or past,
>And the tears no one can hear,
>
>Through my eyes,
>The looking glass of existence,
>Seeing someone else living my life,
>Wondering why that can't be me,
>
>I am told life is measured in moments,
>So I hurry up and wait to be counted,
>With no reflection of thoughts within,
>And no reality of my dream do I find.

This poem was written on 18 January 2017. This poem is about living in the haze of PTSD. There are many types of PTSD and symptoms that go with it.

Living in a haze, where life if out of focus. What would normally be a simple task, can be a frustrating and heartbreaking failure. You remember how you used to be, what you could do. Like watching someone else live your life. Lost in a maze, where today, tomorrow and the past are already forgotten.

In the haze you are existing, not living. Reclusive in the darkness, so no one can hear your cries. If you are suffering from this or any type of PTSD, get help, I did. I was in the haze for about 2 years, don't waste time in your life in the haze.

Tragedy

The Tragedy of war
The endeavor to discover,
That which is unknown in what we do,
On the other side of hell,

The tragedy of war,
Only the fallen will understand,
The brutal demoralization of life,
The tears of blood falling for all time,

The tragedy of war,
The crusade to the end,
A warrior of chaos to be,
The searching of dreams to find life in the darkness of war,

Those who have marched by rank and file,
Have sacrificed for the cause of peace,
They bear the burden of that is peace,
Have earned my respect for all time,

Where are they now,
Those who shall never return from the conquests of war,
The future of all man,
The debt we now owe,

Come forward you masters of death,
Leave behind the walls from which you hide,
I can see behind the mask you wear,
Your absence has defined your appeal for all time,

War is the feast of death,
The devouring of youth and innocence,
Mankind must find an end to war,
Or war will find the end of all man.

This poem was written on 3 October 2017. This poem is about war, and the tragedy that is war itself. War is a brutal demoralization of life, and only the dead have seen its end.

One of the biggest issues I had when I was deployed on my combat tours, was the visits from our "elected" officials. They want to come out to see the troops, but that's not really the priority of their agenda. Disclaimer, I cannot speak for all the "elected" officials that came to Iraq and Afghanistan, only the ones I met.

One a couple occasions in Sadr City Iraq, we had some "visitors" come and want to meet the troops, or so we were told. The real agenda was to get their pictures taken at "The Wall", where the Battle of Route Gold happened. The place where we sealed off the enemy from shooting rockets into the Green Zone in Baghdad. This area was also home to the Jamella Market, the largest open air trade market in Iraq.

My problem with these people, they never served in the military, they will send you to your death, and smile for pictures afterwards. They can fool some of the people, but they can't fool the truth.

I am not afraid to go to war, but I believe if we are going, we should fight to win. Our elected officials should be there too, so they can see the horrors of war. Maybe then we will see an end to the senseless loss of life. For if mankind doesn't find and end to war, war will find the end of man.

THE LAST WAR

Cries of the Warrior

None are visible,
But they are in great abundance,
Tearing apart the hardened heart,
Leaving only the emptiness of present,

No one sees the pain,
The dark consuming thoughts,
The spirit fleeting,
Leaving only the demons of defeat,

Unchanged in the eyes of everyday,
The wounds do not reveal,
The breaking of a soul,
The essence only known to one's kind,

With every daggered word,
Echoes of life burn throughout the mind,
Reality engulfs one's nature,
And so begins the end,

Sadness creates its strangled hold,
With no path seen to what was,
The sum of being is now faded,
But the stains still remain,

Constant is the battle,
Between remembering and forgetting,
The silent villain of the dark,
The storm in which the fury rages,

Cries of the Warrior,
Shed unseen from the hardened heart,
Suffering unspoken,
Abandoned in the barrenness of life.

This poem was written on 28 March 2017. This poem is about the true feelings of a warrior. They make look hard and rugged, and they are, but they have a big heart that loves very deeply those close to them. They are hardened by training and war, but can be wounded very deeply by their pointed words.

You cannot see the pain, because they will never let you see their pain. For only those who have lived like they lived, and walked like they walked, will ever understand, the talking of the talk. That may sound funny, but trust is a big deal with us. If you are not in the circle, circle of trust that is, you are an outsider.

The echoes of life are burned into their mind. For what they can remember that is. It is a constant battle of remembering, and forgetting the same thing. It's very hard when you remember being the warrior, and not being able to remember much about being a warrior.

Warriors do cry, but you will never see it. Their hearts and minds are hardened by years of training and war. They love with all their being, but suffer in silence from the wounds inflicted closest to them. Why do we do this? because that's how we protect you from the real horrors of the world. We never want those closest to us, to see what we've seen. And we will deal with it for the rest of our lives.

The Last War

I am back on the ground again,
Tour of duty number four,
My body still broken,
The blood and dust I can still taste,

Dwell times a year they say,
But the hard times keep coming,
Still burdened with thoughts that should be forgotten,
On the last war I am still fighting,

We fight with our own convictions,
As we try to maintain a sense of normality,
Until the trigger springs,
And you no longer can,

The stress of war consumes you,
Its deadly tension slicing across the mind,
Your hands grip the weapon tightly,
Just itching to flip the switch,

We perfect ourselves as weapons,
As our conscience slowly fades,
We sharpen our ideals to a razors edge,
To justify the violence we proclaim,

You can see it in our eyes,
We still have the stair,
Gazing upon the horrors past,
Imprinted upon the vision of today,

War is personal,
It holds you captive,
Even after it has ended,
The silent screams still pierce the core,

We go to war the first time,
Invulnerable and invincible,

But we all come home with demons,
Some we burry deep inside,
While others climb their way into your soul,

We have seen the horrors of war,
And faced the fear of death,
This is the battle we still fight,
Trapped inside the last war.

This poem was written on 2 November 2017. I wrote this poem about experiences in my Army career and life after the military.

When I was a 1SG in Germany, I was honored to serve with Company A, 1st Battalion, 6th Infantry Regiment. We were called "Raiders". Our Brigade had returned from Iraq in November 2006 and was already scheduled to return a year later.

Most combat deployments are slotted for a one year period, and when you return to your home station, you have a one year reorganization period called "Dwell Time". Dwell time gives units the ability to rest, refit their equipment and personnel. That sounds great right? One whole year not deployed, one whole year off. Yeah right!

Because of the operations tempo for deployments to both Iraq and Afghanistan, Dwell time usually consists of 5 days of re-integration training (basically helping you get back to life out of a combat theater), 2-3 weeks of leave, and 10 ½ months of training to go back to war. Yes that's right, dwell time does not mean lots of time for rest and relaxation. You go right back to work preparing for war.

One key thing I realized during our train up for the next deployment was the level of aggression my Soldiers had during training events. It was if they were still back in the fight, and had no sense that we were back in Germany training. The more I observed the Soldiers and myself, I realized we were still fighting the last war. Don't get me wrong, and an Infantry leader, you want your Soldiers to be aggressive, but not to the point that they cannot differentiate training and combat.

I love my Soldiers and still do. Even though I am retired, I still think of them as mine and miss the days we were a team. Despite all the patriotic themes, Soldiers (Marines, Airmen, Sailors etc.) fight for their brothers and sisters to the left and right. They are your family, and your conviction to fight is for them. I was honored to serve with these men and would gladly fight by their side any day. We are Brothers, we are Raiders for Life!

When you return from war, you try your best to get back to a normal life, sleeping in a real bed, eating real food, no one shooting at you or trying to blow you up. The stress from combat can consume you and it's not like a light switch, you cannot just turn it off, so when that stress is triggered, its game on. You go from peaceful and quiet, to

100% combat mode. The problem with this is you do not see the changes in yourself or your actions of being aggressive. This is how we have been trained for years, and it is engrained in our minds.

This is what I was noticing about my Soldiers and myself. They had that look in their eyes; they were bringing the horrors of the last war and implementing them into the training. We were very aggressive, to the point where I had to stop training, and do some decompressing. They were so amped up, the stress triggers from the training scenario put them right back into the war. I wanted them to be aggressive, but also be able to know when and where to turn it on.

When you train for war, you sharpen your skills to be as lethal as possible. So when the fight happens, you inflict as much violence of action as possible. When you deploy for the first time, you believe you are invincible. Went through my first two deployments without a scratch, then wounded a few times on the next two. The physical wounds will heal, but the emotional wounds that everyone brings home are a different story.

We are taught to conquer all emotion, fear. You learn to bury it deep inside, to show no weakness. You have to do this so you can function in combat. The only problem with this theory, eventually the horrors from combat will come back. Noticed I said "WILL" come back, not may. Some you can learn to bury and forget, but others will come back. And when they come back, it can change you forever. There is no timeline for this phenomenon; it could be days, months or years after combat. So many of my brothers and sisters are at this point in their lives, the demons have comeback and they are still fighting the last war.

For my brothers and sisters who are out there still fighting, it's not a sign of weakness to ask for help. I eventually did, and it helped me tremendously. Don't wait for it to happen, go now. You have to learn to let it go, you don't have to fight the war any longer. It will take time believe me, but you don't have to be trapped any longer. Do it for yourself, do it for the ones you love, just do it!

Picture taken in September 2006, Ramadi Iraq
What was left of my HMWV after the IED strike

ABOUT AUTHOR

Michael Morton is a freelance writer and Poet. He has work forthcoming in Leadership, Poetry about PTSD, Inspirational Poetry and Life Lessons for Little People, children's stories that promote values and morals . He is retired from the U.S. Army and served numerous combat tours in Iraq and Afghanistan. He is a recipient of the Purple Heart, Bronze Star Medal for Valor, and Army Commendation Medal for Valor. You can visit his website at www.angelsthreeproductions.com

www.ingramcontent.com/pod-product-compliance
Lightning Source LLC
Chambersburg PA
CBHW042341150426
43196CB00001B/9